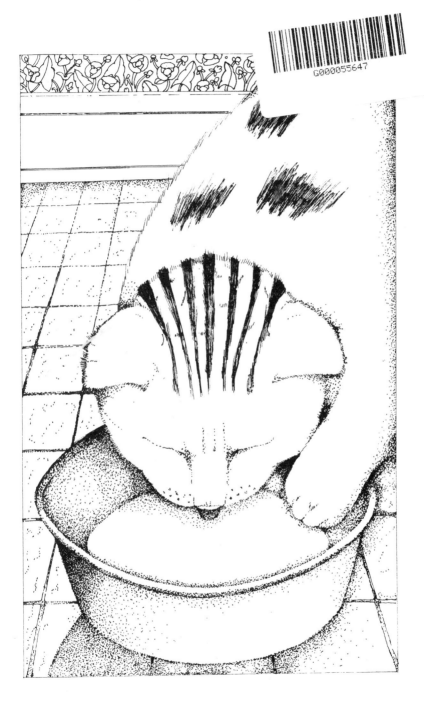

Good Food for Your Cat

Jean Powell

Illustrated by Linda Douglas

CITADEL PRESS   Secaucus, New Jersey

Library of Congress Cataloging in Publication Data

Powell, Jean.
  Good food for your cat.

    1. Cats—Food. I. Title.
SF447.6.P68   636.8′085   81-4300
ISBN 0-8065-0766-7   AACR2
ISBN 0-8065-0769-1 (pbk.)

First American edition, 1981
Copyright © 1980 by Jean Powell
All rights reserved
Published by Citadel Press
A division of Lyle Stuart Inc.
120 Enterprise Ave., Secaucus, N.J. 07094
Originally published in the United Kingdom
by Pelham Books, London
Manufactured in the United States of America
by The Book Press, Brattleboro, Vt.

ISBN 0-8065-0766-7 (hardcover)
ISBN 0-8065-0769-1 (paperbound)

Contents

THE IMPORTANCE OF CORRECT FEEDING

Good Diet Means Good Health

Only a well fed cat can be a healthy and happy cat. A badly nourished body easily falls victim to many ailments and it is as important for a cat to get the sort of food it needs as it is for you. Wrong feeding (which is not just starvation, but may include over-feeding, especially with the wrong foods) lowers a cat's stamina and resistance to disease and saps his vitality. Proper food in the right amounts, neither too much nor too little, and the chance of exercise, are essential for good health.

What is a Balanced Diet?

Not everything that helps to comprise a good balanced human diet is of the slightest use to a cat and his special dietary needs must constantly be borne in mind. Because these are so different from ours he cannot just be fed on table scraps. The preparation of a good fresh diet for a cat will take a little care, time and money, though if you are willing to go to this trouble you should be rewarded by a fine healthy animal, who will bloom far brighter on well chosen fresh foods than he could on the processed contents of tins.

WHAT DOES A CAT EAT?

Your cat's dietary requirements vary from yours in several respects, the basic difference being that a cat is a carnivore (a meat-eating animal) and man is an omnivore (he eats all sorts of things). A cat's teeth are different from ours: they are sharp and cusped, adapted to tearing flesh. A cat does not masticate on smooth molars as we do: its food gets quickly lacerated into shape and then disappears with indecent haste. It does chew its food more than a dog does, but does not grind it as we do. The tongue, with its spoon action, plays an important part in feeding, but the slack lips do not.

Herbivorous animals (those eating leaves and grass) have long intestines to aid difficult digestion; those of carnivores are short, and that of a cat exceptionally so. The cat is more of a true carnivore than a dog: a dog can happily be fed on a diet which is half cereal, but a cat needs meat and very little else. One of the peculiarities of the feline diet is the exceptionally high demand for protein, and the lack of any genuine requirement for carbohydrate and roughage. The amount of food needed by a cat is far greater, bodyweight for bodyweight, than that needed by a dog.

Another peculiarity is that the cat is able to cope with a very high quantity of fat in its diet and apparently thrive on it. One frequently reads in older books that cats should be fed only on lean meat, but modern experiments have proved that this is simply not the case. Unless a cat leads a very sedentary life and is overweight, a natural amount of fat in its diet will do more good than harm.

Cats have long been "civilized", but in their natural state their food would consist mostly of rodents, small rabbits and birds, eaten with the complete garnishing of skin and fur, and even some feathers. The vegetable contents of the stomach would probably also have been swallowed, adding a little important variety to the diet. In addition, cats occasionally, like dogs, eat grass as an emetic, though this has no nutritional function.

Under the unnatural conditions arising from its long and often lethargic history of cohabitation with man, the cat has learnt to adapt its diet to some extent: it will usually no longer live solely on meat and water, though, while it likes some variety, the extra foods it is prepared to consider are far less catholic than those accepted by a dog. There are many stories of depraved felines hung up on titillating extras such as chocolate ice-cream, curried mushrooms or strawberries, but such tastes are not normal.

In addition to natural foods such as red meats, fowl, rabbit and offal, most cats like fish (a traditional but not really a primary food for cats), milk (not natural for adult cats, but good if it agrees with them) and any other foods of animal origin, such as egg and cheese. In addition, they will frequently learn to accept a small vegetable or cereal addition to their diet. A diet consisting of meat alone may be lacking in certain dietary elements, in particular calcium, though I have known a series of strappingly healthy elderly cats who would not deign to touch anything but meat, offal, fish and *milk*. However, it is painfully expensive to feed a cat on animal protein alone, and if you can get him to accept a pollution of up to 25% of vegetable and cooked cereal matter in his food, so much the better for you, though fat cats ought not to get too much carbohydrate, and no cat can cope with a lot of roughage.

It is always best to train a cat to accept the diet you consider best for him right from kittenhood, though changes may be attempted later if they are introduced gradually. A cat not used to eating vegetable or cereal foods should have them added to his favourite food in very tiny amounts at first; then gradually increase the additions. However, don't offer him new foods which you are not convinced will do him good, just because they are cheap. It is better to give him less food but good food, and a *variety* of good foods. Don't spoil him by indulging his preference for just one thing: for the sake of his health he must accept a varied diet.

FUSSY FEEDERS

To most dogs food is food, to be examined by the stomach rather than the nose and brain, but cats are among the world's most fastidious gourmets. Their mealtime fads are notorious. If you have one of those placidly well-adjusted treasures who will regularly eat what is offered with relish, consider yourself fortunate and spare a thought for many an insulted chef who will set before a hungry young tom a sparkling dish of fresh liver (his favourite food until yesterday), only to see him peevishly attempt to cover it up with imaginary earth from the kitchen floor. Most cats are eccentric about food at least occasionally and some may suddenly for no good reason reject a hitherto favoured food and never again touch it.

Once you know something about feline nutrition, you will be in a more impartial position to decide what is best for your cat than he is; you are also bigger than he is, so try to win the battle of wills over the dinner dish. However, it is necessary to bear in mind the somewhat abstruse peculiarities of feline make-up which affect a cat's response to what it is prepared to eat. The cat is a very discriminating and particular animal whose senses are highly responsive to the smell and taste, and even to the appearance and texture of its food. It is very quick to detect any unapproved additions, be they ever so minute. It will also get very set in its ways from an early age.

11

When you get a new kitten you need to ask the previous owner what it has been eating and continue that same diet at least for the first few days, until he is settled; sudden changes can cause tummy upsets, though this may not mean that they are unsuitable if introduced slowly. If you consider the kitten's old diet to be inadequate, inconvenient or lacking in variety (or not suited to the cat's particular likes and dislikes, which, within reason, ought to be taken into account), then introduce gradually any changes you deem necessary, but remember that a cat is a rigidly conservative creature which only likes the foods it knows, and you must start as you wish to go on. It is extremely difficult to get an adult cat to break habits formed in the first three months of its life.

If introduced to new foods at an early enough age a cat can, however, prove remarkably omnivorous. Most adults will drink cow's milk because they are introduced to it as kittens; many caught young will also enjoy vegetables and cereals, or other unnatural foods. However, it is important to remember the cat's exceptionally high demand for protein, which it prefers to be mainly of animal origin: most cats will express little interest in a low protein diet. On the other hand, some good quality animal fat in an otherwise unpalatable diet may increase its acceptability.

Once a young cat is settled into a good, varied routine which suits him, be firm and try to keep the upper hand. Never offer any food which is anything but absolutely fresh (cats are justifiably revolted by meat which is even slightly off), but if a finicky cat refuses a meal which you know is wholesome don't relent and give him something else. Leave the food out for half an hour: sometimes a cat, seeing that nothing more fitting to the whim of the moment promises to appear, will, under slight protest and pressure of hunger, make do with what is there. If he does not, remove the offending food and let him wait till the next meal. A few hunger pangs concentrate the mind wonderfully. However, such methods should not be pushed beyond a certain point as even hunger will frequently not force a cat to eat a food he has set his heart against, even though it is something another cat would relish. After food of one sort has been rejected and a meal skipped, offer him some *new* fresh food at the next meal which you know he likes, and he will probably be less difficult.

If meals are frequently refused, satisfy yourself that, on the one hand, the animal is not being offered foods to which he is allergic or adamantly averse and, on the other, that he is getting enough variety

in his diet to whet his appetite and that the rejection of a favourite meat is not just due to the fact that he is insufferably fed up with being given the same thing day after day with little relief. It is true that cats are often greedy for foods they particularly like, but avoid the temptation of indulging such whims. Their health may suffer and they may eventually lose their taste for an over-indulged luxury.

The temperature at which food is fed is also of great importance to a cat, which may reject a wholesome offering because it is too cold or too hot. Food straight from the refrigerator is unpalatable to a cat and may cause digestive upsets. The ideal temperature is blood heat: anything warmer is also less acceptable.

Cats will frequently be put off their food if they have any reason to feel insecure. They are creatures of habit and may be upset by a strange or a dirty bowl; by their dish being placed in a different position; by too much light or noise; by the presence of strangers. Cats badly disorientated by being moved to a strange place sometimes refuse to eat altogether. Cats who are the only animals in a house are generally more fussy than members of a group who will need to take what's going before it's gone; but the same thing is of course true of children.

HOW MUCH FOOD DOES A CAT NEED?

If a cat frequently refuses meals, it may be that you are feeding him too much and too often. Unlike a dog, an adult cat usually knows when he has had enough. Similarly, if a meal is left only partially eaten, serve a little less next time. Overfeeding is harmful and a cat should not be allowed to get into bad habits.

However, it is not usually necessary to be too rigid about the size of meals offered: just as you, for no real reason, may feel hungrier on some days than others, so will a cat. If he goes through a period of refusing food, which may be related to some psychological disturbance, then just offer a very little at a time. On other occasions, especially in cold weather, you may find him a seemingly bottomless pit. Unless he is overweight, a cat may safely be allowed more latitude in deciding how much he needs than a dog, though with small kittens the intake of food should be more carefully controlled.

Although the amount of food a cat needs each day may vary, it is good to have some basic idea of how much he can be expected to need. As a general rule, it is usually stated that you should allow 50 calories or $\frac{1}{2}$ oz of food a day for each 1 lb of his body weight (15 g per .45 kg), so that a cat weighing 8 lb (3.6 kg) should need 4 oz (115 g) of solid food a day, or 200 calories, milk being fed as an extra. However, that any healthy and even moderately indulged cat would consider this enough for two filling meals is doubtful. Whereas the $\frac{1}{2}$ oz to 1 lb ratio is well enough for most dogs, for whom it is also suggested, it does not provide more than a subsistence ration for most cats, who need proportionately more food than dogs.

It is impossible to lay down firm rules about how much food a cat will need; requirements are greatly influenced by weather (an animal will eat more when it is cold), sex (a neuter will need less than a sexually active male or female), way of life (a cat free to roam over a wide area will eat more than a soporific one kept in a confined space), age (a young animal will need more than an old one) and individual metabolism (some bodies simply need more food than others because they burn it up more quickly). A young or middle-aged neuter, or a male or female not actively breeding, who does not lead a particularly adventurous life and who weighs about 8 lb (3.6 kg) would probably need at least 285 calories a day for normal bodily maintenance. This is more like ¾ oz of food to every 1 lb of bodyweight (20 g per .45 kg). The 200 calories a day of the ½ oz to 1 lb rule might be suitable for an elderly neuter of languid lifestyle. However, even 285 calories would not be sufficient for an active young male, and nowhere near sufficient for a pregnant or nursing female. Also, during the vital early period of quick growth and energetic activity, food requirements are very high. A cat will do most of its growing in the first six months, and by nine months it should appear adult. However, growth will usually continue at a much slower rate till it is eighteen months old, and during this latter period food requirements will be proportionately higher than for a fully grown adult. After eighteen months, when complete physical maturity has been reached, food needs will level off at a lower food-to-bodyweight ratio: a cat should not gain weight after this. Later, food requirements will decrease with failing activity in middle and old age.

The 285 calories a day required by the "average" cat will be composed of protein, fats and some carbohydrates, but it is important that at least 20% of these calories come from protein. If the food is low in protein the cat's appetite may be satisfied before he has had enough protein to satisfy his real bodily needs.

If a cat is healthy and has good teeth and a keen appetite he will probably dispatch an appetising meal in a couple of minutes. Unless it is something which requires a lot of gnawing and picking, he should certainly eat all he needs in ten minutes and anything left after that may be considered surplus to requirements and removed. The only other general rule about amounts to be fed is simply to weigh your cat

once a month: if he loses weight he can't afford to lose, but is otherwise healthy, you are not feeding him enough; if he gains weight after eighteen months of age and cannot be offered the option of exercise, you must feed him less, especially less carbohydrate. However, occasionally neuter cats grow into 20 lb monsters through metabolic disruption rather than overfeeding and there is little that can be done about it.

The Danger of Obesity

A fat cat is not a well fed cat; it is a badly fed cat. A well fed cat is sleek and slim and active. Overweight brings lethargy, and overfeeding can be far more harmful than underfeeding. The first indication that a cat is in less than perfect health is the effect on its fur and skin, and it is interesting that overfeeding, the supplying of an excess number of calories, may result in a poor coat and susceptibility to skin infections, things which tend rather to be associated with underfeeding.

Though cats are, on the whole, better judges of their requirements than dogs, there are always greedy cats, especially pampered and sheltered elderly neuters with little chance of exercise and little on their minds but food. Some will happily consume two or three times their actual requirements and continue to grow and grow and grow — unless interrupted. At the risk of bruising a tender personal relationship you will have to check an expanding waistline with a determined cut in rations — which will no doubt be resented as enforced starvation. You cannot explain it to a hard-done-by cat, but comfort yourself with the thought that overweight shortens an animal's life, causes fatty degeneration of vital organs and increases its liability to heart and kidney diseases.

However, before one starts making any drastic cuts in rations one should study the *quality* of the cat's food. It is possible for an animal to be overweight and yet undernourished: many cats are fed far too much carbohydrate in their diet, and correspondingly too little protein. If you know that your cat's diet has been poor, start by simply improving its quality rather than drastically reducing the quantity of food given. Gradually increase the protein content, offering moderate quantities of fresh lean meat, liver or fish, and offer fat sparingly and carbohydrate only in the form of a little milk. If canned foods are used, make sure you are not using a kind which has a high carbohydrate content, as many of the cheaper ones do. It is wrong suddenly to enforce a crash diet; the reduction in the amount of food must be gradual and must be accompanied by an improvement in quality. Frequently just the improved quality does the trick. Even if it does not, it is important to ensure that an animal is in otherwise good health before you start depriving him of food.

If you are convinced that the quality of your overblown cat's diet is excellent, it is probable that you are simply giving him too much. Before you begin the slimming down process, try to calculate what you think he *ought* to weigh. This may be anywhere between 6 lb (2.7 kg) for a small-boned cat and 12 lb (5.5 kg) for a large-boned cat. Then allow no more than $\frac{3}{4}$ oz of food for every 1 lb of this desired bodyweight (20 g to .45 kg). If a tubby cat weighs 9 lb (4.1 kg) but is small-boned and may reasonably be desired to weigh only 8 lb (3.6 kg), then allow only 6 oz (170 g) of food a day, split between two meals, and let this be good lean meat, offal or fish with just one small saucer of milk a day as an extra. However, changes in quantity ought to be introduced gradually.

If, after four weeks, your cat is as fat as ever, slowly work down to the $\frac{1}{2}$ oz of food to 1 lb of bodyweight rule (15 g to .45 kg), making sure that vitamin and mineral supplements are used to ensure that the nourishment provided is of excellent quality. It is probably not advisable to go beyond this point, though some experts recommend one drastic week of near-starvation. Most owners would prefer a plump cat.

19

HOW MANY MEALS DOES A CAT NEED?

In its natural state the cat is an occasional feeder rather than a continuous feeder like a sheep or even a regular one like man. The wild cat relies on the luck of the hunt. However, the domesticated cat has been happy to adapt himself to frequent, regular feeds.

An adult cat over eighteen months old can manage on one good meal a day, especially in summer, though if it fits your schedule to give two, morning and evening, this does avoid the worst excesses of anxious clamour from an over-hungry cat. But be consistent: have set times for meals and whenever possible stick to them despite the fact that most cats' clocks run fast. A greedy cat will soon get the upper hand once he discovers he can coax an indulgent owner into feeding him whenever he considers it appropriate. His means may be the most winsome: a friendly rubbing against your legs, with tail held high, and a lot of purring. It is hard to resist; but if you are firm about meal times right from the start a cat can be suitably programmed.

The advantage of giving one meal a day rather than two is that a cat will probably then be hungry enough to eat what is offered without being choosey. The large evening meal can be supplemented with just a saucer of milk, or milk and biscuit or porridge, for breakfast. You must arrange the cat's feeding programme to suit yourself. However, when a cat gets older it is better to give two small meals a day rather than one large one. Certain other classes of cats (kittens, young cats and pregnant or lactating females) also require more than one meal a day because they need more food, but all these special cases will be discussed later.

20

THE CONSTITUENTS OF FOOD

The basic elements which food contains — protein, carbohydrates, fats, vitamins and minerals — are all essential. All must be given, though not in unlimited quantities.

Protein

Next to water, protein is the most abundant material in the animal body, accounting for half of the dry weight. The largest proportion of this protein, about one-third of the total amount, is to be found in muscle tissue (such meat therefore being, as food, a very rich source of protein), while one-fifth is contained in bones and cartilage, one-tenth in skin and the rest in other tissues and fluids.

The animal body needs to renew its supplies of protein constantly: body tissues need to be repaired all the time and fluids need to be supplemented. During the vital period of growth in young animals (and also, in later life, during pregnancy and lactation) the demand for protein is increased as the animal needs to synthesise new body tissues (or, in the case of lactation, milk, which is high in protein). In old age, on the other hand, the need for protein decreases.

Proteins are composed of amino acids which combine in different ways to form different proteins. About one third of these score or more of amino acids are "essential", which means that they cannot be synthesised by the animal himself. These are indispensable and must be given to him in his food. If he gets these, he is able to make the others in his body. Some foods — meat, milk, eggs and yeast for instance — provide all the essential amino acids and these are called complete proteins. Foods which are incomplete proteins need to be combined with other foods containing other amino acids so that complete proteins are formed before these can be used in the body-building process.

There are two types of protein, animal protein and vegetable protein. As all the essential amino acids are to be found in both, it is at least theoretically possible to feed any animal on a vegetarian diet. However, it is animal protein which is the natural and favoured food of the cat and it is the more readily absorbed and used. The chief sources are meat and fish, and, to a lesser extent, milk, eggs and cheese.

As we have already seen, the cat has a particularly high demand for protein, best satisfied by a plentiful supply of fresh raw meat. Somewhere between 20 and 30% of a cat's calorie intake should ideally come from protein — more for a kitten and a little less for an older cat. The protein requirement of an adult cat has been stated to be approximately 5 g of protein to every 1 kg of bodyweight — or a little more than ¼ oz for each 2¼ lb of cat. A cat will not *enjoy* meals which are low in protein.

In addition to its primary functions of building and repairing tissues, excess protein, which cannot be stored, is used to provide some heat and energy, a function also performed by fats and carbo-hydrates. A well exercised animal will certainly require more protein than a sedentary one, though this is largely due to the fact that there is more repair work to be done in a well-used body.

In order to use protein properly for building tissues, it is necessary for the body to have a source of energy — to have a certain intake of calories, though in the cat's diet these are best provided by fats rather than carbohydrates.

Carbohydrates

Starches and sugars are a cheap and important source of calories for most animals and they are found in most foods. The cat, however, is unusual in having no actual need for them. It can, though, make some use of them as an energy source.

The cat's digestive system is not so well equipped as man's to cope with starchy foods: we need to chew such foods well to mix them with the digestive juices of the saliva, which help to make them digestible, but a cat does not masticate so carefully, or have the same sort of saliva as we do. A cat just gives its food a quick chew to reduce it to small enough pieces to swallow; the difficult task of breaking down the starch is left to the digestive juices of the stomach and intestines. In order to be absorbed, starches must first be changed to sugars by the action of enzymes.

In addition to starches and sugars, cellulose is also a carbohydrate, though it is in fact indigestible. It is important for most animals as roughage, but the cat requires very little fibre and so does not need cellulose. Cats will sometimes eat grass, but this serves as an emetic and not a food.

Carbohydrates which are not needed immediately to supply energy are stored, some as glycogen in the liver, the rest as fat, which can be drawn upon when energy needs exceed the intake of calories.

It is not necessary from a cat's point of view to supply deliberate sources of carbohydrate in the diet, though most foods contain some carbohydrate and milk has a substantial amount. A cat that regularly drinks milk should not get too much carbohydrate from cereal sources, though it may suit the owner's pocket to introduce some cereal foods into its diet: carbohydrate is cheap and protein is expensive. When a cat is fed carbohydrate in solid form it is usually as grain foods, sugars being less advisable as they are bad for the teeth. Such cereal foods should be cooked as the starch granules are broken down by the heat of cooking and thus more easily digested. Whole wheat flour is included in some of the recipes below, and if the cooking time of the meat is short the flour should be previously baked.

Fats

Fats are composed of the same elements as carbohydrates — carbon, hydrogen and oxygen — though not in the same proportions. They are the most important source of energy and energy storage, providing twice as much energy as equivalent portions of carbohydrates. They are oxidised in the body to produce heat, which maintains the body temperature. In the tissues of the body, fats act as protection for muscle tissue, nerves and vital organs. Like carbohydrates, however, fats have no building function.

As already mentioned, the cat is unusual in being able to tolerate and thrive on very large quantities of fat in the diet. Fatty foods have the advantage of satisfying the appetite for a relatively long period as they remain longer in the stomach. The fat in the food coats particles of protein or carbohydrate so that the digestion of these is delayed until the intestine is reached and the film of the fat is broken down. By slowing the passage of food, fats aid the digestion.

A deficiency of fat in the diet may lead to abnormal skin and fur development and may encourage skin infections, whereas a cat with an adequate supply of fat in his diet will have a healthy and shiny coat. Adequate supplies of fat will be obtained from a variety of meats, fish and whole milk.

Vitamins

There is much still to be learned about vitamins and what is known is already so complicated a subject that it is difficult to set out feline needs with any degree of simplicity or accuracy. All animals, however, require all vitamins for the growth and proper functioning of their bodies and need to get most of them from their food, though the amounts needed and the amounts they are actually getting are not always possible to determine. The various vitamin deficiencies have many consequences, some dire in acute forms, especially where deficiencies occur in early life. First to suffer are usually the health of fur and skin, while a deficiency may bring the added problem of inappetence (lack of appetite), which will worsen the condition. However, the animal fed a good balanced and *varied* diet with the recommended supplements should get adequate supplies of vitamins.

Vitamins fall into two major categories: the water soluble (the B complex vitamins and C), which are not easily stored in the body, and the fat soluble (A, D, E and K), more easily stored, and which demand some fat in the diet in order to be absorbed. Unlike man, the cat is capable of synthesising Vitamin C in his body and he does not need to get it from his food; in addition, Vitamin D is required from food only in small quantities, mostly in winter, as it is manufactured by the action of sunlight on the oils of the cat's coat and taken in when the animal licks itself. Other vitamins, however, need to be supplied in the diet. Plentiful in foods such as meat, fish, milk, eggs and unrefined grains, some vitamins are destroyed by heating, preserving or long storage.

Cats have a high demand for Vitamins A and B1 (Thiamine). Liver is a particularly good source of Vitamin A, as is cod liver oil, but over-feeding of Vitamin-A-rich foods can be harmful as the excess is stored. Cats which eat huge amounts of liver may absorb too much Vitamin A which, in extreme cases, may result in bone deformities. Cats are unusual in not being able to make use of carotene, the precursor of Vitamin A: they must be given the vitamin itself.

Vitamin B1 is very easily destroyed by heat but can be added to the diet in the form of, again, liver, or Brewers' Yeast. Cats are usually particularly fond of Thiamine-rich foods. It is not stored in the body and so there is no danger of excess.

Minerals

The principal minerals, calcium, phosphorus, sodium, potassium, sulphur, magnesium, iron, chlorine and iodine, are all present in the body in measurable amounts. They are absorbed into the cells and fluids of the body and are all in some way essential for bodily functions. In addition to these there are also trace elements, manganese, copper, aluminum, zinc, silicon, fluorine and cobalt, the importance of some of which is today questioned, which act as catalysts, having an effect on other substances in the body without actually undergoing any change themselves. They are usually found in the body in exceedingly minute quantities.

As with vitamins, it is not usually possible to know the amounts either needed or given, but a balanced varied diet of fresh foods should be sufficiently rich in most minerals for a healthy adult. The possible exception is calcium, the most important dietary mineral, which is so necessary for healthy teeth and strong bones. As almost all the calcium in the animal body is contained in the bones and teeth, a diet of muscle meat and offal alone will be deficient in this mineral unless it is supplemented by some calcium-rich food, as commercially prepared pet foods are. Ground bone or feeding bone flour (*not* gardeners' bonemeal) are useful additions to a cat's diet, especially if it does not have milk. A cat which drinks large quantities of milk, however, will probably be getting an adequate amount of calcium. The minerals calcium and phosphorus need to be absorbed in the proportion of six to five so that it is necessary to see that an animal which is given extra calcium (especially important in kittenhood, pregnancy and lactation) is also given almost equal quantities of phosphorus. Fortunately milk and the special calcium-rich compounds which one can buy commercially contain both.

THE IDEAL DIET

A cat should get a good, varied balanced diet, very high in protein and low in carbohydrate and starchy roughage, with adequate supplies of fat, minerals and vitamins. In practical terms this means that, ideally, his diet should consist of at least 75% of a wide variety of types of meat and offal, including some good quality fat, supplemented by fish, milk and small amounts of the vegetable and cereal foods recommended below. Vitamin and mineral additives may on occasion be desirable, especially to ensure that supplies of calcium and Vitamin A are sufficient. Such additives are especially important to growing cats and breeding females. Even if milk is given regularly, water should always be made available.

A 7 lb (3.2 kg) "average" cat should be given between 150 and 250 g (approximately 5-8 oz) of meat (or fish) a day, supplemented by 30-60 g (about 1-2 oz) of cereal, potato or rice and 100-200 ml (about 3-6 oz) of cow's milk. In addition, unless proprietary foods which already contain additives are used, and especially if muscle meat only is fed, it is recommended that the diet is supplemented by 2-5 g ($\frac{1}{10}$-$\frac{1}{5}$ teaspoon) of sterilised bone flour. In addition, one or two yeast tablets or a proprietary vitamin and mineral supplement is suggested.

RECIPE IDEAS FOR ADULT CATS

Meat

It is a hard fact when prices are rising so quickly that meat is fast becoming a luxury even for man that this precious substance is the basic and almost exclusive food of cats, perhaps relieved by the occasional substitution of fish — also expensive. However, this need not always be the sort of meat which you or I would eat without protest: a cat's standards are a little different from ours. It is important, though, that the meat be fresh and wholesome.

A Good Chew

When preparing meat for a healthy young cat with good teeth, remember that his teeth are there to be used. Meat need not be pulverised to a paste or cut up into something resembling mince except for a kitten or old cat with poor teeth: a young adult can cope with larger chunks. Soft food is swallowed without chewing and tartar may build up on unused teeth, causing bad breath and decay. In its natural state a cat would need to put in a fair bit of toothwork on gristle, bones and fur. A young boudoir adult with good teeth can manage surprisingly large pieces of meat, including skin, gristle and even, unlike a dog, most uncooked bones.

Raw Meat

Most cats or kittens, if given the choice from the start, will prefer fresh raw meat to cooked any day. Raw meat is also better for them, having lost none of its taste, juice and natural salts; it is suspected that raw meat has certain properties, beneficial to cats, which are destroyed by cooking.

Freezing

Keeping fresh raw meat on hand all the time is no longer a problem as most households have, if not a deep freeze, at least a refrigerator with a freezer compartment which is sufficiently good for short-time storage. If you buy a pound or two of a few different kinds of meat from your butcher at a time, cut them into meal-sized portions, wrap them individually, and freeze them, you will find that feeding a cat on healthy raw meat, its natural food, is little more bother than opening a can.

However, it is important to remember that freezing does not destroy the action of bacteria in food as canning does, but merely suspends it; as soon as meat is defrosted it is liable to start going off. The other important thing to bear in mind is that frozen meat, once it has been allowed to thaw, should never be re-frozen (unless it is first cooked; but it is better to use it immediately). Obviously one needs to take as many careful precautions when handling meat for an animal as when it is destined for human consumption.

It is essential that frozen meat is completely defrosted and warmed to blood heat before serving; an animal should never be given meat straight from the refrigerator even if it has not been frozen. If you have a hot oven handy, frozen meat can be quickly defrosted by baking for a few minutes: it is not necessary to leave it in the oven long enough to cook it.

A Variety of Meats

Animal flesh (innards, skin, the lot) is exceedingly rich in protein, vitamins and most minerals; unquestionably it is the most valuable food you can give your cat. But remember that the natural food of a carnivore is the whole carcass, torn apart, fur and all, and don't be too fastidious about what sections of animal anatomy you are prepared to offer. Variety is also important and most types of meat are perfectly acceptable: veal, mutton, horseflesh, chicken, rabbit; muscle pork is rich and a little suspect but won't hurt now and then.

Beef

Beef is traditionally considered the best meat for cats: if you can get any which by some stretch of the imagination could be called a cheap cut, your cat will do well on it, with the help of a few supplements. Various beef innards (as mentioned below) are good and often cheap, though muscle beef is particularly rich in protein. Cheaper cuts such as stewing steak, shin, skirt flank or beef cheek are worth trying. If you have the freezer space they may be bought in large quantities.

Bones

One does not normally associate bones with cats, yet, like dogs, they have teeth which benefit from use, and which bones help to keep clean and strong. A nice smooth marrow bone which tempts a dog will not hold the same fascination for a cat, though a piece of raw meat straight from the animal, bones and all, and even fur, can provide much enjoyment. Though great care needs to be taken with certain foolish individuals, cats are usually better at handling bones than are dogs and most can cope with an uncooked chicken or rabbit carcass: a cat is a careful feeder who will meticulously examine its food with nose and tongue before tackling it.

However, do not feed a cat small brittle bones such as cooked chicken or rabbit bones; cooking makes bones crack and chip easily. Brittle bones can splinter and scratch or cut the mouth or throat. Small bones may also become lodged between the teeth or in the gullet, though once they reach the stomach the cat's gastric juices can, within an hour and a half, make them pliable and safe. Fish bones are also dangerous.

Breast of Lamb

Lamb or mutton is usually popular with cats. Breast of lamb may be served raw. Just cut in large chunks, without removing the bones, and leave the cat to exercise his jaws by biting out the bits of meat and cartilage (which is rich in calcium).

Horse Meat

If you can get it, horse meat is an adequate food, but it does go off very quickly and should not be fed raw if it is even slightly suspect. It tends to be on the tough side, which a cat with good teeth likes. Do not feed too large a ration, or too often, as it may cause indigestion.

Chicken on the Bone

Unlike dogs, cats can usually cope with raw chicken bones. A complete segment of chicken, or an unwanted uncooked chicken carcass, is frequently a great favourite and will keep an initiated cat happy for a long while. However, cooked chicken bones, which become brittle, may cause problems.

Chicken Heads and Gizzards

Most butchers will give away chicken heads if asked. If nice and fresh they may be given to the cat just as they are, feathers and all, and will provide a good long chew — preferably out of doors.

Chicken Feet

Though low on actual food value, these also provide a good deal of amusement to the initiated cat.

Rabbit on the Bone

Cats usually adore rabbit. Like chicken, its bones are brittle when cooked, but in raw chunks it is a great delight to most cats. However, nowadays rabbit is frequently bought in a frozen slab — which needs thorough defrosting before being served.

Cheap Cuts

Nowadays they are often not readily available, but the cheaper animal parts are the most useful to pet owners: things like offal, melts, paunch and gristly bits of meat. Lungs are not high in nutritional value but are very cheap and usually popular with cats. More expensive but excellent value are heart, liver and kidneys, all extremely nutritious.

Beef Heart

The heart is a muscle and the good solid muscle meat of beef heart or the hearts of smaller animals which one can buy is extremely high in protein. Beef heart is usually the best value and very highly regarded by most cats. Do not discard any blood clots in it, or the large arteries and veins which emerge from the top: they are all good food.

Lamb or Pork Hearts

Lamb hearts are usually more expensive than beef heart but some

cats seem to like them even better. Pigs' hearts are also good: imported frozen ones can sometimes be bought from big supermarkets quite cheaply.

Liver

Liver is the most nourishing of all meats and will satisfy the cat's high requirement for Vitamin A. However, one must resist the tendency of some cats to become addicted to liver to the virtual exclusion of all else: Vitamin A is toxic in excessive amounts as it is stored in the body, and an all-liver diet has been known to result in a painful condition called hypervitaminosis A. However, in normal and even large amounts liver is in no way toxic, though raw liver should not be fed too often (probably no more than twice a week) as it is a laxative. Instead of a meal consisting solely of liver it is a good idea to mix a little liver with some other meat. Cats love its taste and will appreciate it even in very small amounts. All types of liver are good; beef liver is particularly good value considering its high nutritional content.

Kidney

This can be a bit expensive, though beef and pork kidneys are good value and very nourishing. They are best fed raw if good and fresh, cut in chunks as large as your cat can manage.

Melts

Melts (spleen) is a good cheap meat, which may be fed raw, though it is not very high in nutritional value. Be careful about giving it too often, however, as, like liver, it can have a laxative effect. Mixed with some other meat it is a good standby.

Lungs

Don't be put off by their disgusting appearance: most cats adore lungs. They are not high in nutritional value, however, so are best served together with a more nourishing meat such as liver or beef heart. On their own they are adequate for a breakfast for a cat which does not really need breakfast but thinks he'll have it anyway. A portion needs to be judged on weight rather than size as raw lungs are largely air and what may look quite a sizeable amount is really very little. The fact that they are extremely cheap certainly makes them worth keeping in the freezer.

Fat

As we have seen, cats can thrive on fairly fatty meats and a little extra fat or butter, or the oil from a tin of fish, can often make a meal more desirable. However, moderation should be shown if a cat is overweight, and most cats will not relish fat in large lumps.

Cooked Meat

Sometimes meats are better served cooked than raw, especially if you are not quite certain of their freshness. Cats are almost always very particular on this point and won't touch meat that is even slightly off. If you think it is a little borderline, then cook it lightly and leave your cat to decide upon the success of this operation. One should not condemn him as a fussy nuisance if doubtful meat is rejected: unless you are convinced that refused food is completely fresh then give him the benefit of the doubt, and credit for a more sensitive nose, and let him have something else.

Some cats, and especially older cats and small kittens, are not good at handling bones, and cooking has the advantage of facilitating the removal of bones and bone chips. It also makes the removal of excess fat easier: though the cat is able to cope with large amounts of fat there are limits, and cheaper meats are frequently extremely fatty.

Older cats with poor teeth may find raw meat difficult to cope with unless it is minced or very finely chopped; cooked meat is easier to chew so that tough meats may be cooked to advantage if you are feeding a senior citizen.

Finally, some cats simply prefer cooked meat to raw. However, it is best to feed raw meat at least twice a week.

When meat has been cooked, always be sure to allow it to cool to blood heat before serving. A small quantity of some vegetable or cooked cereal as recommended below may be added to an all-meat meal. If nutritional supplements are added this should be done only after the food has been allowed to cool.

In some of these recipes stock or broth is useful in cooking, and methods of preparing these are to be found on p.51.

Methods of Cooking

Baking. Roasting or baking is a convenient way of cooking meat if you have a hot oven handy and do not have to pre-heat it specially. If just partial cooking is required, it is sufficient to place the meat on an open oven-proof dish with a little butter, fat or vegetable oil on the

bottom to prevent sticking. If longer cooking is required, the dish will need to be covered with a lid, or a piece of buttered paper or foil, to prevent it from drying out too much. Otherwise first melt a little butter or fat in the dish and roll the meat in this before cooking: this both prevents too much drying out and adds to the palatability of the meal. If you have the oil from a can of sardines or tuna this may be used when baking either meat or fish.

Boiling. If meat is boiled, keep the liquid to a minimum so that there is very little left by the time cooking is finished. This liquid should never be thrown away as it contains a great deal of the goodness from the meat. A small quantity of stale whole wheat breadcrumbs or cooked brown rice may be added to the meat to help soak up the moisture, or some of the liquid may be used with future meals, or served on its own as a soup.

Frying. Most cats enjoy meat fried in a little butter or fat, or the oil from a can of fish. But meat should never be overcooked.

Grilling. If meat is grilled it may be necessary to add a knob of butter or fat to prevent it from becoming too dry.

Other methods of cooking may be tried in addition to these (e.g. steaming), but the above are usually the simplest.

There follows a series of cooked meat recipes. Some are more convenient to prepare in far larger quantities than a cat could eat in one day, but the additional portions may be individually wrapped and stored in the freezer.

Skirt Stew

Cut the skirt in pieces and place in a saucepan with enough cold water to cover. Bring to the boil and simmer for an hour. Remove all bones carefully.

Baked Bread and Meat

Take 2 thin slices of buttered stale whole wheat bread and at least ½ lb (225 g) of any meat or offal scraps. Place one slice of bread, butter side down, at the bottom of a greased oven-proof dish, cover with pieces of meat and place the second slice of bread, butter side up, on top. Pour over a teacupful of stock or water and let it stand for an hour, then bake for 30 minutes in a moderate oven, keeping covered.

Beef and Egg Fricassee

Any oddments of raw or cooked beef are suitable. Simmer in ½″ of stock or broth for 5 minutes, then remove from the heat and stir in an egg (which need not be beaten first). Mix well and return to the heat for 3 minutes.

Hotch Potch

Take about 1 lb (450 g) of scrag end of lamb and a calf's foot, both cut in pieces. Place in a saucepan with enough cold water to cover, bring to the boil and simmer for 2 hours. When almost cool, remove the bones.

Boiled Neck of Lamb

Place the neck of lamb in a large saucepan and just cover with cold water. Bring to the boil and simmer gently for an hour. When almost cool, remove the meat from the bones.

Fricasseed Breast of Lamb

Cut a breast of lamb in pieces about 1″ square. Place in a saucepan with just enough stock or water to cover and simmer gently for 15 minutes, or long enough to allow any bones to be removed. Add a tablespoon of baked whole wheat flour, mixed to a paste with a little cold water, and cook for a further 5 minutes.

Meat and Giblet Casserole

Take about 6 oz (170 g) of any available meat scraps, cut in chunks, and dredge with whole wheat flour. Place in a greased oven-proof dish. On top of this spread chicken or turkey giblets cut in pieces. Pour over ½ teacupful of stock, cover, and bake in a moderate oven for 30 minutes.

Stewed Beef Liver

Raw liver has to be fed in moderation as it is a laxative. Cooked liver frequently has the opposite effect and is therefore a convenient alternative. Cut the liver into chunks and dredge with whole wheat flour. Fry lightly in a little butter or fat, then transfer to a saucepan containing ½″ of stock. Do not simmer for longer than 5 minutes.

Baked Liver

Beef liver is usually the best buy, but any sort may be used. Cut into 1 ″ squares and dredge each piece with whole wheat flour. Place on a greased baking sheet and sprinkle with whole wheat breadcrumbs. For an exceptionally nutritious dish, the breadcrumbs may be mixed with a beaten egg. Bake in a moderate oven for half an hour, partially covered with buttered paper or foil so that the liver does not dry out.

Roast Liver

Any sort of liver may be used. Leave it in one large piece. Take an oven-proof dish lined with foil greased with a little butter, fat or vegetable oil. Place the liver on this and raise the edges of the foil so that they almost completely cover the meat. Cook in a moderate oven for half an hour, or less if partially cooked liver is required.

Fried Liver

Cut the liver into conveniently sized pieces which, if you wish to add a little cereal food to the meal, may be dredged in previously baked whole wheat flour. Fry in a little butter or fat until just cooked.

Stewed Beef Kidney

Cut 4 oz (115 g) of beef kidney (or other kidney) into strips. Dredge a little whole wheat flour over them, and fry in a little butter or fat for a couple of minutes. Pour over them enough cold water or stock just to cover and stew for 20 minutes.

Baked Kidney Custard

Place 4 oz (115 g) of sliced pork kidneys (or other kidneys) in a greased oven-proof dish. Mix together one beaten egg, ½ pint (235 ml) milk and 2 teaspoons of whole wheat flour, and pour over the meat. Cover and bake in a moderate oven for 30 minutes. When almost cool, cut in slices.

Stewed Melts

Prepare as for Stewed Beef Liver. For a more wholesome meal use equal quantities of melts and liver.

Roast Melts

Cut ½ lb (225 g) of melts into pieces and place on a greased baking sheet. Cover with butter paper or a little tin foil and bake in a moderate oven for half an hour. For a more wholesome meal, use equal quantities of melts and liver.

Stewed Beef Heart

Stuff the heart with 2 tablespoons of stale whole wheat breadcrumbs or an equal quantity of cooked brown rice if desired, but do not remove any clots of blood which are there. Place in a large saucepan, the broad end of the heart upwards. Pour over 1 pint (473 ml) of water or stock. Bring to the boil and simmer gently for 2 hours. When almost cool, cut in pieces. This will be enough for many feeds and extra portions should be individually frozen, each with a small quantity of the bread or rice if used.

Beef Heart Casserole

Cut the desired quantity of beef heart into fairly large chunks. Place in a casserole dish with ½ ″ of stock or water and bake in a hot oven for 20 minutes, or until just cooked.

Baked Lamb Heart

Slit the heart halfway open, if desired, and fill with 2 teaspoons of stale whole wheat breadcrumbs, moistened with enough stock or broth to make a dough. Place on a greased baking sheet, cover with buttered paper or foil, and bake in a moderate oven for half an hour. When fairly cool, cut in chunks.

Cold Weather Special

Mix together two parts liver, one part melts and one part oatmeal porridge cooked with milk. Warm in a slow oven so that the meat is partially cooked.

Stewed Sheep's Tripe

The bleached tripe usually sold by butchers is not suitable for cats as the preparation used to whiten it may cause stomach upsets. Unbleached tripe, however, is useful if you can get it, and adds variety to the diet. It contains less protein than muscle meat but is easily digested. It should be carefully washed and is best served lightly boiled. Simmer for half an hour in a little water, stock or milk after cutting in pieces.

Roast Tripe

Cut the tripe into 2 oblong pieces. Mix a small beaten egg with a tablespoon of stale whole wheat breadcrumbs. Place one piece of the tripe on a greased baking sheet and spread the egg and bread mixture over it. Cover with the second piece of tripe, then roll up this sandwich very lightly, and tie. Cover with buttered paper or a small piece of foil and bake in a moderate oven for an hour. When almost cool, cut in slices.

Chitterling Hash

Chitterlings (small intestines) are tasty although not greatly nourishing. Chop into 2″ pieces and simmer in $\frac{1}{2}$″ of stock or water for 15 minutes. Remove from the heat and stir in an egg (which need not be beaten first). Mix well, then return to the heat for 3 minutes.

Chitterlings and Liver

Use equal quantities of chitterlings, cut into 2″ pieces, and beef or other liver, cut into 1″ cubes. Simmer for 15 minutes in $\frac{1}{2}$″ of stock or water.

Stewed Brains

Cut the brains (any sort will do) into large sections and place in a saucepan with a little water or stock, mixed with a small amount of whole wheat flour (about 1 heaped teaspoon to $\frac{1}{2}$ lb [225 g] of brains). Simmer gently for 20 minutes.

Boiled Beef Tongue

Raw tongue can be very tough, but cooked it makes a good dish. Put the tongue into a large saucepan with enough cold water to cover. Bring slowly to the boil and simmer for about 3 hours: a large tongue may need even longer. When almost cool, cut in generous chunks, keeping any remaining liquid as stock.

Stewed Calf's Feet

Divide each calf's foot into 4 pieces and simmer for 2 hours. Carefully remove all bones when almost cool and put them in the stock pot.

Baked Calf's Foot

Place the foot in an oven-proof dish and cover with 1 pint (475 ml) of stock or water. Cover and bake in a moderate oven for 2 hours. When almost cool, carefully remove all bones and use for stock.

Lamb's Feet

Throw 4 sheep's feet into fast-boiling water and cook quickly for 5 minutes. Drain and allow to cool, then take each foot firmly in the left hand, give the bone a jerk with the right hand, and draw it out. Cut the hoof from the end of the foot. Boil the bones in the liquid to make a rich stock.

Stewed Pig's Trotters

Take 2 pig's trotters and split each in half. Place in enough boiling water to cover and simmer for an hour. Cool and remove the bones.

Stewed Ox Tail

Cut an ox tail into 2″ pieces at the joints. Put the pieces in a saucepan with cold water to cover and bring to the boil. Simmer for an hour. When almost cool, remove all bones, which may be further boiled up in the liquid to make a rich soup. Lambs' or calves' tails may also be used in this way.

Fish

Although it is traditional to feed cats on fish, it is not their natural main diet and is not quite as nourishing as meat. Nevertheless, it is a great favourite with most cats, adds variety to their diet and is a valuable alternative source of protein. It is also easily digested and rich in minerals. However, cats tend to lose their taste for it if it is fed too often and too much fish may produce eczema, digestive troubles and a bad-smelling cat so that it is advisable not to feed it more often than two or three times a week at most. Most parts of a fish can be used, including skins and soft tails, but *not* bones. Cats often like raw fish but be careful of this unless it is perfectly fresh and has been very well filleted. It is probably better for fish to be cooked as it is then much easier to remove the bones.

Methods of Cooking Fish

Steaming. Steam it in a double-boiler with a little water or milk, then shred the flesh from the bones.

Boiling. Boil just long enough for the bones to be easily removed. Use only very little water, and the remaining water should not be thrown away or much of the goodness will be thrown out with it. A little cereal food may be added if it is too moist.

Baking. Place on a greased oven-proof dish and bake in a moderate oven for 5 minutes, or until the flesh comes away from the bones.

Frying. Fry lightly in a little butter or fat until just cooked.

Types of Fresh Fish

Both lean types of fish such as cod and haddock and fat fish such as herring and mackerel may be used, though most cats would prefer the latter. The flat white fish which we value most highly, such as sole and flounder are not usually a cat's favourite; he likes something a little more robust and strong tasting — and smelling.

Fish Scraps

Fishmongers are often only too willing to give away fish scraps, heads and bones, though the time and unpleasant labour involved in boiling these up and carefully picking through the stew in an attempt to separate the bones from the fish is often off-putting. The smell of cooking such fish is totally obnoxious by human standards, though it drives cats delirious and the evil looking mush which results is usually a great favourite.

Pressure-cooked Fish Bones and Heads

A less tiresome way of dealing with fish scraps, heads and bones is to cook them in a pressure cooker until the bones are soft and may be crushed to a pulp with the oddments of fish which adhere to them. This makes a good meal, very rich in calcium and other minerals.

Boiled Fish Bones

If you have fish bones with very little flesh on them, and no pressure cooker, and can bear the smell, the bones may simply be boiled in enough water (starting from cold) to cover. Simmer for as long as possible, but for at least 2-3 hours. After cooking, strain to remove all bones. The liquid, when cool, should form a tasty jelly.

Boiled Cod's Head

A large cod's head may contain quite a lot of flesh, which makes it worth the trouble of cooking. If you have to pay for it at all, it will not cost very much. The bones in the head are large and easy to deal with. Place the head in a saucepan with just enough cold water to cover. Bring to the boil and simmer until the flesh falls away from the bones, which should be carefully removed when cool. If it has been boiled long enough, the rest will set to a nutritious jelly. If it remains rather liquid, a few stale whole wheat breadcrumbs or a little puppy meal may be added.

Canned Fish

In addition to various proprietary brands of canned fish for cats you might sometimes be prepared to sacrifice a little of your own varieties, which often go down well.

Tuna

There are some reports of canned tunafish being harmful to cats, though if you can spare a teaspoonful as an additive to a meal it will probably be appreciated and do no harm.

Sardines

A cat will usually consider a can of sardines a luxury, though the oil may cause diarrhoea if too much is given. The oil does, however, have the beneficial effect of helping to prevent hairball by lubricating the hairs swallowed by the cat when washing and so helping their passage to the stomach and through the intestines.

Mackerel

Many cats enjoy canned mackerel, which is wholesome and considerably less expensive than tuna or sardines.

Canned Cat Foods

Certainly many household pets have benefited from modern convenience foods, which are the products of much research into animal nutrition. The pet food business is a multi-million-dollar industry which is highly competitive and the best pet foods on the market are unquestionably useful. You can feel confident that a *good* cat food

46

(which usually means one of the more expensive kinds) will provide the sort of nourishment your cat needs, having been specially designed for that purpose.

With the best will in the world, an owner might not always know what is best for his pet. This problem is not helped by the fact that a cat frequently has very definite ideas himself about what is best for him — and he is not always right. A cat easily becomes addicted to a deficient diet: having once proved his *penchant* for one particular food, he may wish to eat that to the virtual exclusion of all else. With a good proprietary cat food at least a balance of elements is provided.

However, it is unwise to rely entirely on canned food. Cats appreciate variety, and there is nothing better for a cat than a good balanced diet of different fresh foods: he will certainly prefer such a diet to a boring regime of canned food. Nevertheless, convenience foods are a godsend and a cat should be trained to accept them as a standby and an added source of variety: served two or three times a week, alternating with good fresh foods, they help to provide a balanced diet. If your cat shows no enthusiasm for cans after being brought up on fresh meat, try mixing just a small amount of canned meat with a favoured fresh diet at first, increasing the amount as he gets used to the new flavour.

Opinions vary as to how good various canned cat foods are. Certainly many cats live exclusively on them and apparently do well, though breeders often claim that, to be in really tip-top condition, a cat needs fresh meat. One definite drawback of canned foods is that they tend to offer a cat too little to chew, and a cat does like variety in texture. Certainly some commercial cat foods are better than others, having a higher protein content, and correspondingly less carbohydrate. Cats need a diet of 20-30% protein, as we have already seen, but it is only the best cat foods that will supply this need adequately: some contain as little as a quarter of this percentage of protein. The vitamin and mineral contents of different commercial foods also vary greatly. Vitamins and protein are frequently destroyed during the preparation of these foods, though artificial supplements are added to make up for this loss.

Dried Foods

Like canned foods, commercially prepared dried cat foods which come in pellet form are a useful standby but should not be relied upon too much. When these are used it is vital that a plentiful supply of fresh water is available to the cat. Alternatively, dried foods may be soaked in hot water, milk, stock or broth. When fed dry they are useful in helping to keep a cat's teeth clean and strong. Some cats will also eat dog or puppy biscuits, which are equally beneficial.

Table Scraps

To help ensure a varied diet there is no harm in including certain table scraps in your cat's food, though they may not all be to his taste. Some cats will not even touch meat which has been seasoned, and no cat should be obliged to eat what clearly does not suit him. However, if you have scraps which you consider suitable, they are worth trying. Most meat and fish oddments may prove acceptable if they are not too highly seasoned, and some cats like egg, cheese, cereal foods, porridge, milk puddings and certain vegetables. Avoid, in addition to spicy foods, anything with a lot of sugar in it, and do not offer white bread or biscuits, cakes and pastries made with white flour. Non-foods such as tea and coffee which contain stimulants are also to be avoided.

Eggs

Egg is not a natural food of cats, though they sometimes like a mixture of egg and milk, or a little egg mixed in with a meat meal. Egg yolk is exceptionally nourishing and is an excellent source of Vitamin A; it is useful in feeding tiny kittens.

Cheese

Some cats like a little cheese now and then and it is a good protein food. If your cat has a taste for it, a small amount of grated cheese mixed with a meat meal adds variety to a diet.

Cereal Foods

Though the addition of cereal foods to your cat's flesh diet is not essential, some may be used, but they should not comprise more than 25% of the food. Only cooked cereals are useful: cooking makes them more easily digestible. And only whole grain and not refined cereals should be used. If a cat is overweight it is best to eliminate the cereal part of the diet completely, while even a lean cat can cope with very little carbohydrate and roughage. Below are some suggested cereal foods which may be tried:

Stale whole wheat breadcrumbs
Feeding bone flour
Puppy meal
Puppy or dog biscuits, crushed
Cooked brown rice
Flaked corn
Barley kernels
Cooked oatmeal or oats porridge
Cooked whole wheat macaroni or spaghetti
Any other cooked whole grain cereal food

Vegetables and Fruit

It may be argued that vegetable matter is a natural food for cats, in small quantities, as in their wild state carnivores would be likely to consume the half-eaten contents of the stomach of their prey. Domestic cats, whose prey is usually offered on a saucer, are therefore thought to benefit from a little added vegetable matter. It is not easy for them to digest, however, so it is best if it is finely chopped and cooked; and the taste is usually not greatly relished so it is wisest to offer it discreetly disguised with the meat. If you start such doubtful practices when a kitten is small you will probably get away with them. It is extremely unlikely that a cat would suffer any ill effects through not eating any vegetables, but as they are commonplace and cheap there is no harm in trying.

Some cats actually like particular vegetables. Carrots and other root vegetables tend to be the least despised. Too much potato may prove indigestible, though some cats eat mashed potato as a regular part of their diets and seem to thrive. Other vegetables worth trying are peas, beans, lentils, parsley, broccoli, lettuce and turnip tops: as a rule cats are not keen on green vegetables, except perhaps spinach, though you may successfully infiltrate a little cabbage without causing a disagreement. Just a teaspoonful of one of these vegetables two or three times a week is adequate, unless a cat actually likes them.

As an alternative, cats sometimes like raw fruit or fruit juice, in particular tomato or tomato juice, and sometimes have even more exotic tastes for things like grapes or oranges.

Milk

It is traditional to give cats milk and most, though not all of them, prefer it to water. Cow's milk is much less rich than the milk of the mother cat, which means that it is not the best thing for small kittens, but their special requirements are discussed later. For most adult cats it is adequate and provides valuable extra protein, vitamins and minerals. One pint (473 ml) of milk contains as much protein as four eggs or 3 oz (85 g) of meat. It is an especially good natural source of calcium, important for healthy bones and teeth.

Some cats — Siamese in particular — will not take milk (though cream may be a different matter). Among those who do like it are some individuals who cannot digest it properly because their digestive juices lack certain enzymes which would normally convert lactose, the natural sugar in fresh milk. When lactose remains undigested there is an accumulation of fluid and fermentative bacteria in the intestine, resulting in persistent diarrhoea. In such cases the amount of milk given should be reduced, or excluded from the diet altogether, unless the cat will accept as an alternative sour milk or yoghurt, in which the lactose has already been converted. Some cats are very fond of these. If a cat does not have milk in any form it is important to supplement his diet with vitamins and minerals, and in particular to supply an alternative source of calcium, such as bone flour.

Even with cats who can normally digest it, large quantities of fresh milk will sometimes make the bowels loose. It is best to stop the supply if a cat is suffering from diarrhoea; but do see that he has water. Alternatively, boiled milk, or a mixture of boiled milk and water, may be given, as this has a slightly constipating effect.

Cats often like evaporated milk but this frequently causes diarrhoea, as does full-cream powdered milk, because of the high lactose content. Skimmed powdered milk is, however, safe.

It is sometimes claimed that one should not feed meat and milk at the same meal as this can cause digestive upsets, but this is not always a problem.

Stocks and Soups

The following may be fed on their own — they are useful for kittens and a cat recovering from an illness — or used in cooking, or for moistening a very dry meal. Salt and other seasonings should not be used in their preparation.

Basic Meat Stock

Any unwanted raw or cooked bones are suitable for this, as well as cooked or raw skin, gristle and trimmings of meat, poultry and offal. Simmer in plain water — about 1 quart (just under 1 litre) water to 1 lb (450 g) bones — for as long as possible on a low heat with the lid on. Most of the flavour will be extracted from the meat in the first 2 to 3 hours of simmering, though more gelatine and calcium will be drawn out of the bones and meat if they are boiled longer. After cooking, carefully remove all bones and bone chips, best done by straining.

Meat Broth

Any left-over cooked or uncooked scraps of meat, gristle, skin or bone may be used, but avoid anything highly seasoned. If you are buying meat specially to make broth, a calf's foot is very suitable. Simmer for 2 to 3 hours, using about 1 quart (just under 1 litre) of water to 1 lb (450 g) meat and bones. After cooking, carefully remove all bones and bone chips but leave in the scraps of meat, skin and gristle. If you are using a whole calf's foot, it will need to be simmered for as long as 6 or 7 hours, topping up the water when necessary.

Fish Stock or Broth

Proceed as for meat stock or broth, but be specially careful about removing all bones.

Water

Water is not a food, yet it is the most important of all the elements in any animal's diet. A creature can survive without food for a surprisingly long time, but must have water constantly. The cat is basically a desert animal which needs to drink little water as such, deriving most of what it needs from its food: for example, more than half the weight of meat is water. Milk is largely water, and a cat that drinks a lot of milk may seldom be seen to touch water. Nevertheless, fresh water should always be provided, and replenished at least twice a day to keep it clean. Though cats do not perspire in the way that people do, or pant like dogs, expelling moisture in those ways, they do need a steady supply to carry away the waste products of the body.

Supplements

A normal healthy adult cat fed a good varied diet of fresh foods will probably not need supplements, though if a cat does not drink milk, bone flour containing calcium is important, especially during pregnancy. Yeast tablets are good for added bloom and for sharpening the appetite and cats in the know adore them. Alternatively, a little dried Brewers' Yeast adds flavour to a meal. In winter (or all year round for a cat always kept indoors) cod or halibut liver oil is a good conditioner. Any cat that is a little out of condition will benefit from these, or from the specially prepared cat vitamin and mineral tablets available from pet shops and drugstores. These are specially important for growing cats, pregnant or nursing females, or cats recovering from an illness. A cat fed entirely on cooked food would benefit from additives, and in particular from yeast, which supplements deficiencies in the B vitamins destroyed by heat. Doses will vary according to the condition of the animal, but one yeast tablet a day can safely be given to an adult cat, plus $\frac{1}{2}$ teaspoon of bone meal twice a week and a teaspoon of cod or halibut liver oil two or three times a week.

FEEDING KITTENS

Hand-Rearing Kittens

In normal circumstances there is a capable and doting mother to take care of all the kittens' requirements before they are ready to be weaned, but occasionally mothers are inattentive or without milk, or kittens are orphaned. Hand-rearing very young animals is a delicate and specialised operation, and in case of need expert advice should be sought. However, as kittens develop so rapidly, it can also be rewarding.

One can buy special feeding bottles for kittens, though in case of need a doll's plastic feeding bottle will do the job. Cow's milk is not suitable for very small kittens: the milk of the mother cat is extremely rich and high in protein for rapid growth (containing 5% fat and 10% protein). A human baby formula mixed to double strength is usually effective.

The number of feeds needed by very small kittens is somewhat daunting: ideally food should be provided every two hours during the first four days, three-hourly up to two weeks, and, between fourteen and twenty-four days, three-hourly by day but just once at night. After that age the kittens should manage to get through an eight-hour night without food.

The amounts to be fed will depend largely on individual needs, though, as a rough guide, each kitten should be allowed, at every feed, what it will be able to drink in ten minutes. This will be something like 5 cc of milk during the first week, getting up to twice this amount by the third week.

At 3 weeks weaning can be commenced, first by mixing the jelly from a canned cat food with the milk feed in small amounts, or by feeding the kittens whole wheat breadcrumbs soaked in the milk. Even once weaning has started, frequent feeds are necessary. At least 6 are recommended in the beginning, spaced throughout the day, with an eight-hour break overnight.

Milk Formulas for Hand-Rearing Kittens

1 A human baby formula at double strength.

2 1 teacup fresh cow's milk; $\frac{1}{4}$ teacup light cream; $\frac{1}{4}$ egg yolk; 1 drop cod liver oil; $\frac{1}{4}$ teaspoon sterilised bone meal: stir the cream, egg yolk and bone meal into the milk in that order, then add the cod liver oil. The mixture may be kept in the refrigerator and a suitable portion warmed to blood heat at feeding time, and fed from sterilised feeding utensils.

3 Commercial preparations generally intended for puppies are also good for kittens.

4 Mix together 2 tablespoons evaporated milk, 2 tablespoons boiled water, $\frac{1}{4}$ teaspoon corn syrup or glucose and $\frac{1}{4}$ teaspoon of beef extract or bouillon concentrate.

5 Mix together 1 cup homogenised Vitamin D milk beaten into one egg yolk, 1 teaspoon lime water and 2 teaspoons dextrose.

Care should be taken when feeding kittens or cats of any age on full-cream evaporated milk as, because of the high lactose content, it may cause diarrhoea. The same is true of full-cream powdered milk.

Weaning

Weaning will usually start in the fourth week, or possibly in the third for a large litter. If the mother has plenty of milk it need not be hurried and may take its course over a period of two or three weeks, though kittens will usually begin to show an interest in the food provided for their mother from an early age.

The milk of the mother cat is extremely nourishing: small kittens grow at an incredible rate before they start to take any other food. When an alternative source of milk is offered, it should be something richer than plain cow's milk. Human baby foods are useful and one of the formulas suggested for hand-rearing may be used, while below are further suggestions. Only about a teaspoonful should be given at a time in the beginning and the first feed should be offered when the kittens are hungry (i.e. two hours after their last feed from their mother). To encourage a kitten to drink, dip your finger in the milk and hold it against the kitten's mouth: it will soon get the taste of the milk. If you push the kitten's face into the milk you will only discourage it. It is important to remember that all food offered to cats, and especially to young kittens, should be served at blood heat.

When the kittens are used to taking these extra milk feeds once, and then twice and three times a day, try introducing some solid or semi-solid meat and cereal foods, as recommended below, but new foods must be introduced gradually, and just a very little at a time in the beginning. Watch out for signs of tummy upsets. A rigid schedule should be established, with meals being provided at fixed times, for the sake of digestion as well as discipline. A small kitten's stomach is extremely tiny and not capable of holding enough food to keep it going for more than a couple of hours. If too long a period elapses between meals, it will be encouraged to overeat. At the time of weaning kittens which are still being fed by their mother should get four or five small meals a day. If the kittens are getting little or nothing from their mother, as many as six meals should be given by five weeks of age, two or three milk based and three of meat or fish. The kittens are growing very quickly and need constant nourishment. It is usually considered best to keep meat and milk meals separate for fear of digestive upsets. Make the last meal of the day meat or fish as this will satisfy the appetite for a longer period.

Milk Mixtures for Weaning Kittens

1 One of the milk formulas suggested for hand-rearing kittens.
2 Baby rice with a human baby milk powder at double strength.
3 Goat's milk.
4 Powdered skimmed milk mixed very strong, or cow's milk with a little added dried skimmed milk, mixed with any other cooked baby cereal.
5 Milk with a little lime water or glucose.
6 Milk mixed with raw egg yolk.
7 Milk mixed with wheat germ, stale whole wheat breadcrumbs, farina or porridge.

8 Puppy biscuits simmered in milk.
9 Powders specially formulated for kittens.

Solid Foods for Weaning Kittens

1 Lean scraped beef.
2 Shredded cooked chicken or rabbit.
3 Flaked cooked fish. (Fine-grained fish should be used at first as it is easily digestible; it may be steamed in milk.)
4 Solid human baby foods.
5 Scrambled egg, perhaps with a little farina or other cereal.
6 Proprietary kitten foods.

Suggested Additives

These are recommended for kittens of all ages and may be started as soon as kittens are weaned.

1 Yeast tablets ($\frac{1}{2}$ a tablet a day), or dried Brewers' Yeast ($\frac{1}{4}$ teaspoon a day), or one of the specially prepared yeast tablets made for cats and kittens.
2 Feeding bone flour ($\frac{1}{2}$ teaspoon a day with one of the meat feeds), or extra dried skimmed milk (2 teaspoons added to one of the milk feeds).
3 Cod or halibut liver oil (1-2 drops a day with one of the meals, or $\frac{1}{2}$ teaspoon once a week), or a ration of liver once or twice a week.

From Weaning to Eight Weeks Old

Once a kitten has got a taste for meat, which does not usually take long, it is not necessary to give it so many milky feeds, though milk (one of the special mixtures until at least eight or ten weeks and later cow's milk) is a useful supplement throughout life if it can digest it properly. By eight weeks, when the weaning process is quite completed, a kitten should be getting five meals a day, three small milk ones and two larger meat or fish ones, each consisting of about four heaped teaspoons of food. They should be evenly spaced throughout the day and at set times, though they can be arranged so as to suit the owner's routine. The meat should continue to be minced or scraped in the beginning, though as soon as a kitten can cope with slightly larger pieces it should be allowed the chance of exercising its jaws and teeth. (However, it is not till about seven months that it gets its large strong second set of teeth.)

Remember that the cat's exceptional demand for protein, coupled with the fact that your kitten is growing at a very remarkable rate, means that its demand for good protein-rich foods (especially meat, fish and milk) is very high. It is also extremely important at this stage to get the kitten used to as many different good foods as possible: you will not get a second chance to do so once a cat has become set in its ways. It is a mistake to encourage a kitten to eat by only offering it the things it likes best. From this age a kitten should be trained where to find its water bowl when needed, though it may not drink much water if it is having plenty of milk. It is important to see that all feeding bowls are kept very clean: kittens are very liable to digestive disorders.

Two to Three Months

If you acquire a new kitten, it is best to leave it with its mother until it is eight weeks old, though frequently they will be sold or given away at five or six weeks. You should ask the previous owner what foods the kitten has been getting and follow this schedule closely for the first few days so as not to upset the new arrival. After that, gradual changes in timing, amounts and the contents of meals may be made. If you are not satisfied with the quality of the old diet, then it must be slowly improved almost from the start.

Remember that at ten weeks a kitten still has a stomach only the size of a walnut so that frequent small feeds are still required, but the quantity must be steadily increased as he grows. A kitten should not be offered too much food as it may get into the habit of overeating. Any food that is not eaten within ten minutes should be removed. By the end of this period the number of meals should be reduced to four, two milky and two of meat or fish, each of the latter consisting of six to eight heaped teaspoons of food. Try introducing new foods such as a few cooked vegetables into the diet and make sure that the kitten becomes accustomed to eating a wide variety of types of meat and fish, prepared in different ways. Recipe ideas from the adult section should be used. Kittens of this age will be able to cope with progressively larger pieces of meat, and even bones of the sort discussed in the adult section should be offered.

Three to Eight Months

Up to about four months of age the four meals a day should be continued. Between four and six months the number should be reduced to three, dropping one of the milk feeds. By this time the young cat will probably be eating about nine or ten heaped teaspoons of food at each of its meat meals, though many will prefer less at breakfast time and more in the evening.

By the end of this period two meat meals a day should be sufficient, the more substantial one being served in the evening, with perhaps a small saucer of milk at lunch time and bedtime. Remember that a young cat of this age is still growing and needs an increasingly plentiful, high quality protein diet. Most of this growing will be done in the first six months, but it does continue at a slower rate for a further year, during which period the body will fill out considerably and become more muscular and solid. It is usually safe to allow a young growing cat of this age as much food as he will eat at each meal, though he should not be fed between meals, except with milk, if tolerated. It should be easy to tell whether he is getting enough food or not, and if he thinks he is not he will no doubt let you know all about it.

FEEDING A PREGNANT OR NURSING QUEEN

During the second month of pregnancy a cat will start to need extra food, better given as one or two extra meals rather than larger meals which overload the stomach. The new diet must be high in protein and must contain adequate amounts of calcium and phosphorus for bone building: if milk agrees with her the cat should be allowed as much as she will drink. Do not stretch out the normal food ration by simply adding extra carbohydrate: what is necessary is extra meat and offal, and occasionally fish.

During the second half of pregnancy, and during lactation, the need for vitamins and minerals is doubled or trebled and commercially prepared supplements are recommended, as well as something richer than cow's milk (one of the mixtures recommended for small kittens may be tried), bone flour, yeast, cod liver oil in winter, and plenty of good protein foods. During this second half of pregnancy, and during lactation, at least four or five liberal meals a day are necessary, milk being served between meals as an extra. A nursing female may need as much as three times her normal amount of food when suckling kittens, and the extra food should be continued until her kittens are weaned, then slowly cut back until she is down to normal rations soon after all her kittens have departed.

A Special Diet for a Pregnant or Nursing Queen

Mix together 1 teaspoon precooked, fortified biscuit meal, 1 teaspoon dried skimmed milk powder (fortified with Vitamin D, or else add 2 drops of cod liver oil), $\frac{1}{2}$ teaspoon dried yeast and $\frac{1}{4}$ teaspoon bone meal with enough warm water to make a stiff paste. Combine this with $\frac{1}{2}$-$\frac{1}{4}$ lb (225-340 g) of good meat or offal (or occasionally fish).

FEEDING A SICK CAT

A sick, weak and dispirited cat may refuse to eat and drink, though nourishment and, more particularly, moisture, are essential for recovery, as is quiet and warmth. One should not worry too much if a cat refuses food during a severe illness: that is only natural; but it is vital to provide fluid regularly, even if it is only water.

A sick cat on the mend may have lost its sense of smell, which controls appetite, so that strong-smelling foods are useful in tempting it to eat. Salty tastes are often also favoured. Foods offered should be easily digestible and of high nutritional value. A convalescent cat may refuse to take food from its bowl, but may happily "discover" a tasty morsel carelessly left on the table and enjoy it all the more for thinking it should not be having it.

Liquid Feeds for Convalescent Cats

1 Milk with a little Ovaltine.
2 Toast milk, made by pouring a cup of boiling milk over a slice of whole wheat toast, standing till almost cool, and then straining.
3 A small quantity of fine whole wheat breadcrumbs in milk.
4 Milk slightly thickened with arrowroot, junket or cornflour.
5 Thin gruel made from oats or oatmeal.
6 Milk with added cream, or goat's milk.
7 Yoghurt, perhaps with a little honey.
8 The tomato juice from a can of sardines.
9 Stock or broth (see recipes on p. 51).

Solid Feeds for Convalescent Cats

1 Raw or cooked meat chopped fine (start with the cat's favourite).
2 Chicken, rabbit, hare or game, finely shredded, are very tasty.
3 Half cooked liver (especially chicken or turkey liver), cut small.
4 Half cooked kidney, cut small.
5 Sheep's brains, lightly cooked.
6 Unbleached tripe cut small and simmered in milk.
7 The marrow from bones.
8 Grilled ham.
9 Smelly cheese.
10 Lightly cooked fish, well filleted.
11 Strong-smelling fish such as flaked herring or kipper, or sardines in oil or tomato sauce.
12 Shrimps or prawns.

It is specially important, after a severe illness, that a convalescent cat be given the food supplements suggested on page 51. Cats very commonly develop anaemia during the course of some other illness: symptoms to watch out for are general poor condition, lethargy, depression, weakness, paleness of the membranes of the nose, tongue, gums and rims of the eyes and continued lack of appetite. In case of need, expert advice should be sought. No animal will get back to full good health until it starts eating properly.